# Unglobed Fruit

# Unglobed Fruit

Poems by Esther Greenleaf Murer

ISBN 978-0-557-91242-1

Cover photo: Patricia Wallace Jones, detail from "The Belles of Bolinas"

*To my online poetry workshop buddies, without whose encouragement and fellowship many of these poems would not have been written.*

# TABLE OF CONTENTS

viii

# Acknowledgments

Many thanks to the editors of the following periodicals, in which these poems first appeared:

*Able Muse:* À la Carte

*American Religion and Literature Society newsletter:* Deibide for Pentacost; The Prophet

*Autumn Sky Poetry:* Ostinato

*The Centrifugal Eye:* Anthem du Jour; Antiphon; Decluttering; The Fixer; Indoor Sports; A Poem, Anyhow; Rondel on Lines by James Tate; Shine, Perishing Republic; To a Table

*Drunken Boat:* Descort on a Truism

*The Externalist:* Abandon All Hope; Entitlement; 21$^{st}$-Century American Cutup

*Folly:* Little Plastic Hangers from New Pairs of Socks #3; My Last Duke

*Friends Journal:* Mammon his 4$^{th}$ Commandment

*The Ghazal Page:* Agenda; Chocolate Guzzle; Failed Ghazal with Interuptions; Progress

*Guinea Pig Zero:* Bildad

*Interboard Poetry Competition:* Gregorian Sestina; Fall Day in the Park

*Light Quarterly:* Orientation Speech

*The Literary Bohemian:* Escalators

*Lucid Rhythms:* Jamboree; Once the Spelljack; Sylviade

*Mimesis:* Unglobed Fruit

*The New Verse News:* Paradelle: the U.S. Congress and Copenhagen; Sanctuary; Thanksgiving; The Two Prophets

*Pemmican:* All Fall Down; Jeremiad; Little Plastic Hangers from New Pairs of Socks #1

*Tilt-a-Whirl*: Arrgh Poetica; Halo

*Touch, the Journal of Healing*: Blow, Healing Wind

*Town Creek Poetry*: Aftermath

*Types & Shadows*: Death to the Reconcilers; My Dream Conference; The Powers Speak

*Umbrella*: Discovery; Forecast; Ode to a Creature seemingly incapable of Good; Panto; Plot with Epilog

*Unsplendid*: Legacy; Unjubilee

# À la Carte

The salad's bid farewell to muscle tone,
the soup sprawls apathetic in the dish,
the roast is spavined gristle, fat and bone,
the snickerdoodles aftertaste of fish.

The soup sprawls apathetic in the dish,
not caring whether it is slurped or sipped.
The snickerdoodles aftertaste of fish;
at least no one can call them nondescript.

Not caring whether it is slurped or sipped,
the wine lolls nonchalantly in the glass.
At least no one can call them nondescript
who choose to give this restaurant a pass.

The wine lolls nonchalantly in the glass
hinting at bare feet trampling out the juice.
Who choose to give this restaurant a pass
will never be accused of self-abuse.

Hinting at bare feet trampling out the juice,
the salad's bid farewell to muscle tone.
You'll never be accused of self-abuse
for shunning roasted gristle, fat and bone.

# Abandon All Hope....

The only lines in the Federal Building
are disinfomercials. Though I sneak with a ton
of buns and bagels and have not gloves,
there will be wailing sounds and flashing signals.

The Federal Building has a black marble
heart with matching façade. Even as we keep
watch, the message etches itself above the door:
*Lasciate ogni speranza, voi ch'entrate*

—which means "The law shot Tony Speranza,
boy contralto." Outside, the line foams
down the street to the jail for grannies
convicted of being unfit for military service.

# Aftermath

Exiled from the canoe,
the daddy-long-legs
makes an eight-point landing
on the lake. As it picks
its way across the water's
sunlit skin, its shadow
summons a ferocity
of minnows.
                    Its legs
strike out in all directions,
then wilt
like abandoned
disciples.

# Agenda

Strive to finish what you have begun before the gong sounds.
Redo what you have overdone before the gong sounds.

Shear the Angora goats, spin and dye and weave the mohair,
sew yourself a suit of homespun before the gong sounds.

Stun the world of music with a sellout performance
of your suite for harp and helicon before the gong sounds.

Conjure into the void the oozing styes of commerce
with which the land is overrun before the gong sounds.

Turn the universe inside out and watch the threads
quicken into a ganglion before the gong sounds.

Clothe your choicest insights in green and leafy words
that they may enrich the lexicon before the gong sounds.

# All Fall Down

Ring the trembling tocsin. Gad
around the neighborhood in shoals.
The moldering yore glows
rosy in this twilit moment as
a quorum of resurrectionists
pocket their plunder from boneyards
full of ribs and fibulae. In a void
of good intentions, they derange
posies into misbegotten mountains of
ashes, jetsam into jihads of
ashes, clinkers and clunkers, all
we hoped was forgotten,
all the effluvia we meant should
fall off the earth's edge and
down the maw of the cosmos.

# And Now, the Truth

And now, the truth! Here it is,
the one you've been waiting for,
larger than life and
infinitely more satisfying—
a new, improved
eternal verity from Megaton,
the people who cared enough
to garble forth the naked facts
for your discriminating
pleasure.

Why let your waters be troubled,
or your boat rocked
by the riddle of the deep?
Let Megaton cradle you
in the whispersoft ever-so-gently
daring elegance of ultranow
personal space, custom-designed
for oh-so-fastidious you.

Face it: you'll never settle
for less than total satisfaction.
So coddle yourself
in the Amanita-fresh miasma
of new, high-potency
Cloud of Unknowing.
The ultimate experience.
From Megaton.

# Anthem du Jour

O dutiful mendacious spies
that clamber, cave and drain
the syrup fountain, cadging rides
on shovel-suited cranes!
The merry calamari called
cod, shad, stingrays, and me
and groaned, "I've stood enough on wood
-en seats too high to flee."

# Antiphon

Tender unto mine ear, O tend'rest of buttons,
the sinister singsong of singletons.
Thou tinsel'd halibut, buttress of tendrils,
slender tagalong tenderloin
of the buttered beyond;

*domina trixcum.*

O darling dark of morning, mourning
the anticrepuscular spark that betokens
the broken crepitude of forlorn depths,
muscular larks aborning
in bespoke discrepancies;

*de mortuis non est disputandum.*

O starched vinegar of perceptual plasma,
pleonastic starlings garish in septic vines;
startled stanchions purring in sinecures,
vindictive chasms of chiasmus
staunch on haunches;

*harakiri elision.*

# Arrgh Poetica

*(Treinte-sei)*

When I try to write a poem in forms
I know the effort is bound to be intense.
The first thing is to cast aside all norms
regarding reason, logic, meaning, sense.
The sea of sound will buoy up my boat.
Trust the pattern to keep the thing afloat.

I know the effort is bound to be intense.
I know the chance is infinitely slight
that my poem will make a difference
in the cosmic scheme of wrong and right.
Yet though, Penelope-like, I must expunge
each line again and again, I'll take the plunge.

The first thing is to cast aside all norms
or even better, heave them out to sea
and leave the the critics to their teapot storms
of how a poem should or shouldn't be,
as I adroitly sidestep the abyss
of literary fads, and, blithely dis-

regarding reason, logic, meaning, sense,
I mix my styles or metaphors, or both,
combining Langpo with a Gaelic cadence,
and "fuck" with "o'er" and "like, y'know" with "quoth."
My dictionary of poetic terms
will help me iron out this can of worms.

The sea of sound will buoy up my boat—
the crash of consonance, the ripple of rhyme,
and in another line, not too remote,
lapping alliteration forms a chime;
the murmur of innumerable meters
mimes the drowsy dream of lotus-eaters.

Trust the pattern to keep the thing afloat.
Follow whatever course the lines will take
and seize the treinte-sei by its stroppy throat.
O reader, if perchance you're still awake,
behold my *magnum opus* and rejoice,
for I have found my own authentic voice.

# Beside the Dam

typewriters nestle in the branches
of trellised grape vines
releasing margins
in a cascade of tingalings

across the river
lightning scribbles on the skyline
with a fistful of crayons

yet on moondark nights the children
still feel their way over the trestle
armed against oncoming trains
with a bread knife
and the rest of the chocolate cake

# Bildad

*Terrors frighten them on every side,*
    *and chase them at their heels.*
*Disaster is hungry for them,*
    *and calamity is ready for their stumbling.*
*By disease their skin is consumed,*
    *Death, the Firstborn, consumes their limbs.*
                    *--Job 18:11-13*

A dauntful cavy was Bildad the Shoe-Height.
If we took him out of his cage he would wheep and quiver and jerk,
literally scared shitless;
if we set him down on the floor
he would seek refuge under most immediate furniture
and cower there.

Bildad had few adventures in his short life.
One day he went to school and cringed at the children.
One month while we were away
he summered in the wilds of Northeast Philly,
where he ate watermelon
and cowered under a lawn chair on real grass.

And the Lord smote Bildad with boils,
and an abscess in his throat came open
spewing blood and pus.
He screamed and shat with terror at the vet's.
The vet said the infection
would go to his brain.

And then a strange thing happened:
Bildad the Shoe-Height forgot to be afraid.
He became an intrepid explorer.
Every day as his walk grew crazier
he lurched and sidled and swam,
penetrating ever deeper into the house,
yea unto the farthest reaches of the back bedroom.

Then one morning
he lay chill and trusting on my lap;
we said a long goodbye.
Half an hour later he was dead,
gone to that land where none have need
ever to cower again.

We shrouded him in a plastic bag
and entombed him in the freezer.
Our daughter viewed him daily for a month.
Then Daddy took him to the lab
in a tote-bag hearse, with straphanger cortege,
and the mortal remains of Bildad the Shoe-Height
joined those of all the other guinea pigs
and plunged skyward
in a shaft of transmogrifying fire.

# Blow, Healing Wind

Blow, healing wind, wherever you list.
Swirl the sand in magic patterns;
ripple the dunes with mystic runes
that only the birds can read.

Dance, gladsome sand, in time with the wind.
Garb the land in festal raiment;
swaddle the town in a dazzling gown
against her bridal day.

Chastening wind,
the grains of sand are at your service.
Sting the eyes of mighty rulers,
grind majestic rocks to ghostly pillars,
carve your name on the earth!

Use us, O wind, however you will.
Though the task be rough and bruising,
yet we know 'twill leave us rounder,
rounder than before.

# Bonellia

Twin fronds sweep the ocean
floor, winnowing the water.
Their grooved stem winds
and is lost between the rocks.

A larva wafts into view.
Riding the currents brings with it
the thrill of danger, but now
the hour is at hand—an identity crisis
beyond imagining. Now it is time
to settle down.

> O green fronds,
> fan me into your presence,
> let me become a male!
> Let me find that groove, let me follow it
> down, down into the dark
> where new larvae wait for my touch
> to speed them on the perilous journey
> outward.

> I've heard (or maybe dreamed)
> that somewhere there are creatures
> so gigantic and so remote that they can't
> even see the eggs, but must settle
> for raining bombs from above the clouds,
> not knowing or caring whom they will hit,
> or whether the meeting (if meeting there be)
> will result in life or death. How awful
> not to have all the fathers there
> to nudge you into life firsthand,
> and hold you spellbound as they trade tales
> of adventure out in the sea.

But puberty will not wait. If no green fronds
beckon the larva home,
it will perforce become female. Now
the growth spurt begins. For she must shelter
all those fathers and children within her—
more fathers preparing more children
for their time outside, their time
of testing and danger.

No larva, no father
has seen what lies hidden between the rocks.
They know only the dark at the end
of the grooved stem. Does it matter
what the rest of her looks like?
It only matters that within
is life and love and nurture.

O green fronds,
fan me into your presence!
Doom me not to the loneliness
of being forever outside, a mighty
fortress, gigantic and remote!
Let me find that groove, let me follow it
down, down
into the friendly dark. . . .

# Caveat for a Presumptuous Age

Nowadays nobody loves
a prothonotary tetratherium.
"Too many syllables," they cry,
dropping grave accents
in all the wrong places.

Behold instead a paleohippus:
Crack-of-Dawn Horse is his name.
Astride his shoulder, like a government,
sits a smiling don, from whose mouth
proceeds a pair of sharp sabers.

Wherefore beware
of disparaging your forebetters:
dire wolf, mammoth, giant sloth.
Contend, contend if you will
that foregoing is forgetting;

but the fin-de-Miocene fauves, ah!
throve, uncritiqued by upstart
hominids—though some would trace
our lineage to one who seems more rat
than aye-aye: Purgatorius.

# Chocolate Guzzle

All my friends know how I feel about bittersweet chocolate.
They alert me when there's a deal on bittersweet chocolate.

At parties the other guests gorge upon crackers and brie,
while I go in search of a wheel of bittersweet chocolate.

I'll pass on the buffalo chips with guavas, filberts and chevre,
but I yield to none in my zeal for bittersweet chocolate.

When flyfishing on the river, I don't mind catching nothing;
before leaving home I fill my creel with bittersweet chocolate.

I don't go on marches to save the flammulated skink,
but I reckon I'd storm the Bastille for bittersweet chocolate.

All these quirks mirror a mother obsessed with nutrition
who would never let me make a meal of bittersweet chocolate.

# Clandestine Romance

Waiting on the sidewalk,
the postman's lonely mail cart
meets a pigeon, and is smitten.

Each day while the postman
plays junkmail solitaire
in countless vestibules,
the pigeon and the mail cart prink prink prink
up and down the block in single file,
head and letters bobbling in sync sync sync.

The postman reappears. The mail cart
deftly dims its green-and-lilac
sheen, unpouts its pouchfront,
and is again correct in navy blue.

# Clean

I washed my hair and it shrank.
I washed my face and it frayed.
I washed my clothes and they sparkled.
I washed the dishes and they blurred.
I washed the windows and they puckered.
I washed the floor and it melted.
I washed the front stoop and it bled.
I washed my hands of washing
and took the dog to the cleaners.

# Death to the Reconcilers!

*In memoriam : Tom Fox, Christian Peace Teams member killed in Iraq, 2006*

Death to the reconcilers! Don't you know
that being on the team is all that matters?
Dichotomizing is a sport which all
must play. The rules are simple: Just two sides—
us (the people) versus them (the insects).
Swatting them is the object of the game.
To rid the world of vermin—that's the aim.

And now you peaceniks come and try to tell us
that they're *not* insects? That we shouldn't swat them?
You'd take away our sport—but then, but then,
by what rules should we play? How should we live?
How to tell right from wrong, who's in, who's out?
Oh no, the game goes on. Remember first:
Of all the insects, spoilsports are the worst.

# Decluttering

Time to declutter
the shrdlu.
You take the harebells
and tippets,
I'll take the tuffets
and widdershins.

Here's a rounsey.
Out.
Squill?
Save till later.
Marmosets?
Keepers.

Ranter-go-round?
Under the stithy .
Slumgullions, then?
No.
What about the jimjams?
Put them over there, by the forfex.

That's where I put the swipples.
Fine, then, with the codswallop.
And the isogloss?
File it under "syllabub."
But that leaves all these fetlocks.
Toss them in the scuttlebutt.

Do we have to keep all of them?
We'll need them for tiffin.
Can't we use scrum?
Too many lammergeiers.
I give up.
OK, go relax with your gemsbok.

Tomorrow we'll serry
the oldsquaws
into phalangers and
tanyards.
The grandiloquents
sure left a muckle.

# Deibide for Pentecost

Here in the desert a bush,
scruffy wilderness rubbish
surrounded by bats and owls
and the howling of jackals,

burns without being consumed
here in the desert, costumed
in the shekinah of the Lord's
glory spiraling upwards.

Be silent, take off your shoes,
stay attuned to the echoes,
do not think, only submit;
for you have met the Spirit.

# Descort on a Truism

In all this whole wired hallelujanation
there are no ideas but in things.
Brains freeze at the end of a 14-hour day
and it's off to the midnight mall
to pick random inspirations off the shelves,
sweatshop cornucopias
from container ships of Chinese junk,
repositories of Next Steps
to be multitasked, then flushed away
into sludge ponds of torpid truths
with million-year half-lives.

\*

He thinketh best who hath the most
possessions great and small.
Praise fertile frill and furbelow,
praise things from whom all concepts flow.

\*

A man mistook a thing for an idea. He looked at the chihuahua's
miniature iron bedstead with its miniature orthopedic mattress, and
thought: where there's an object there's an exercise. So he used the
mattress as a trampoline and went splat on the ceiling.

\*

```
C A R R I A G E
A               L
L   M I N D     E
A   I D E A     P
B   N E E D     H
A   D A D A     A
S               N
H A Z E L N U T
```

*

No tranquillity but in the meds,
no music but in the boombox,
no coordination but in the joystick.

No Koran but in the shrapnel,
no truth but in the fios cable,
no eternity but in the black hole,

the thingiest thing in the cosmos.

# Discovery

*To make a clam play an accordion is to invent, not to discover.*
*— Wallace Stevens (on Surrealism)*

It goes without saying that a clam
will lie quiet if music be played to it.
But should you thrust a concertina
in between its valves, what then?

Is this that same passive creature
that now flails in counterpoint
to the strange new growth
on its adductor muscles?

The first tentative glubs and groans
become a shifting palette
of quavery hockets and crotchets,
minims and maxims. The music

of those distorted hemispheres
everywhere takes dominion,
taming the slovenly sea
into a pandiatonic blur whose

warped chords, trapped
in a prism of infinite refraction,
mass and carom at four times
the speed of sound on land.

# Dispatch from the Kremlin

Mao,
the Pathet Lao
rightly throw in the hoosegow
drinkers of bourgeois creme de cacao
as well as all who willfully follow the Tao.
The latter especially we disavow,
and certainly don't allow
here in Moscow.
Ciao.

PS. Люблю рублю.

# Disqualified Because....

Prism, railroad, sousaphone:
    inedible.

Poison ivy, statesmanship, salt:
    missing comic touch.

Peach, cormorant, chessboard:
    no security clearance.

Stegosaurus, quicksand, rocking chair:
    illiterate.

Toilet paper, deadbolt, apron:
    can't carry a tune.

Venus de Milo, telephone book, fried egg:
    don't bounce.

Gelatin, mosquito netting, traffic cone:
    lack opposable thumbs.

# Entitlement

Monday the grackles descended on the square.
A subtle gloss on soigné black purred
of bronze and purple as they minced and swaggered,
helping themselves to all the choicest acorns.
Their long tails with understated fans
mocked the unkempt stubs of their city cousins,
starlings in polka-dotted rusty iron,
who tried to mingle. The sparrows and the pigeons
hung around the margins, or took off
for dingier, more secluded urban pastures.

Today, having done our square, the grackles
moved on, bound for the next port of call.
The starlings are cavorting in a fresh
mud puddle, seconded by the sparrows.
The pigeons repose cradled in the grass.
Tomorrow they'll resume their rightful place
as cocks of the walk, with first dibs on crumbs.

# Escalators

*Kabul, 2006*
A shopping mall has opened, full of wonders.
There is a thing here, and into it you put
a card, and in maybe fifteen seconds
money comes out. The locals spend days
yo-yoing in the city's only elevator,
and take pictures of all their friends
riding the escalators.

*Chicago, 1940s*
The mecca of my childhood: Marshall Field's.
While my mother shops, I ride and ride.
Curious about a crowd, she finds
that all those people are waiting for me
to finish coming up the down escalator.

*Gardemon, Norway, 2003*
As we step onto the horizontal strip
that carries us and our luggage from here to there,
a slant-slashed red circle informs us
that on this escalator that doesn't escalate
jumping rope is not allowed.

*Prague, 1988*
In this gray, glum city the escalator
runs down and down to the metro,
deep, steep and swift. Longing
to transmute my terror into hope
for my fellow riders, I shut my eyes
and sing: "The Lord God is at work
in this thick night." I cannot know
that next year the government will fall.

*Heathrow, 1968*
Between flights we stand by the top
of the escalator where my husband
takes movies of cresting bowlers,
headbands, topis, turbans, fezzes, kofias;
miniskirts, granny dresses, lederhosen,
caftans, djellabas, saris—
all the peoples of the earth
rising and rising.

# Failed Ghazal with Interruptions

The mold inside the breadbox doesn't grow anymore.
Why the wallaby wanders she doesn't know anymore.

> flaccid parasols
> droop over tails of peacocks
> concealing splendor

She who once had such skill at three-dimensional chess
can't even win a game of tic-tac-toe anymore.

> muted flourishes
> fall like sandbags on sawdust
> rousing nobody

Once she aspired to write lays like Marie de France.
Now it's not even chic to write a rondeau anymore.

> pearls and persimmons
> draped over gleaming crankcase
> rhomboid rhapsody

She follows sunken silk roads into the rising sun
tracing a wadi whose water doesn't flow anymore.

> scent of piranha
> mimicking the pale murmur
> of birchbark logic

How shall she ransom the saffron music of the spheres?
Grandfather's silver saxophone doesn't blow anymore.

> fatherless dustmop
> flares among the chameleons
> dromedary wine

Esther guzzles ghazals with swift and sharp abandon,
all because she can't scratch her ear with her toe anymore.

> latch-hooked rug design
> only red-green blind can see
> its feelthy peectures

# Fall Day in the Park

In the lapidary light
of the sea, I am a flatfish
prostrate on the floor
of a cathedral, the eyes
on my back attuned
to the coruscation
of corals, polyps, bryozoa
swaying in the current's sunlit blue.

Now on dancing eddies
I levitate in celebration,
vault and sweep and skew,
pitch and bank and camber
a hymn to overarching glory.
Then I sink again, canting
like a falling leaf, and rest

in the mud, where one day soon
my center eye will contemplate
the bare ruined reef while the other,
the wandering one, keeps watch
for the green ghosts hovering
amid the welter of weeds.

# Fantasy Impromptu

A million soldiers march abreast
across the world from east to west.
A million more without surcease
traverse the world from west to east.
And when at length the two ranks meet,
with none consenting to retreat—
then shall each man confront his foe,
salute, and swing, and do-si-do,
grand right and left, and all sashay
from Land of Fire to Baffin Bay.

# The Fixer

Primed with a flask of Rooibos tea
he donned a tent the color of chameleons
and rollerbladed off on his round
of world-saving chores.

He had finished scutching the grommets
and was about to flense the crisps
when a hyrax fell through the stiff orange air,
catapulting the flensing-horn

into the following weekend
where it lay, slipping and sliding
as one might dunk a donut
into the Sea of Mutability.

Lurching from post to pillarbox,
he bespattered the void
with endorphins of paisley.
Cuffs rotated. A lone bicep sneered.

Nine o'clock and all was past and present
as in a medieval dipstick.
Another world saved,
though not the one he'd intended.

# Foreboding

Freons and halons nibble at the calendar. That inkblot in the center is the eye of weeks to come. Subprime workers sprawl before their boxes of telly heads, hearts glazed over.

The president in his prevaricose tie exhorts us to defy the naysayers who threaten firmness at the core. *Come, let us gorge on white peaches, succulent as marble.* Dread sluices the windows.

The earth's belly seethes and roils with a lambent dirge: *Caldera è mobile.* On the sea of pseudotranquillity time masquerades as eternity, muffling the still whisper: *Carpe seism.*

> forty-two polecats
> comb the edges of terror
> in search of wednesday

# Forecast

Remember that June's
the time when the moons
of Pluto are in the ascendant,
and all the tycoons
dress in pink pantaloons
trimmed with gold lace galloons
and count their doubloons,

unaware that eftsoons
the dominant moons
will be Neptune's in the descendant,
bringing monsoons
and simoons and typhoons
down upon those patroons,
picaroons and poltroons—
making all their doubloons
not worth one brass spittoon
against the Götter-impendent
däm-dämmeroon.

# Gregorian Sestina

Wearing a rented tuxedo
one night in Monterey,
I'm sitting with my friend Jimmy
on a state-of-the-art sofa
stirring a cup of miso
with what looks like a platinum spatula.

Jimmy's girlfriend Ella
lives in this fancy condo
with a loft she calls an "entresol"—
oh my deah it's *tres tres*
*chic*, you'd have to look very fah
for anything like this, *mon ami.*

The wallpaper is ramie.
I guess the place is Shangri-la
to her, but I could think of half a
million better uses for all that dough.
But well, bully for her, hooray.
Not my idea of soul.

Well, I sit there and console
myself thinking of my old army
days, especially my buddy Ray
and a goodtime girl named Stella
we picked up in Laredo
one night—she sure was a laugh a

minute, got to swinging off a
chandelier and landed on the console
of the Hammond organ, waving a dildo
in time with—none of your smarmy
dinner music, but a tarantella.
Then we made a foray

outside, offering stray
passersby a puff of a
joint, hoping they'd (*Insh'Allah*)
sing: even with a voice only so-so
one can manage a chorus of "Mammy"
or caterwaul a glissando.

I'll take doughty graty voices
singing meaty fatty salty ballads
any day over Ella's tra-la-latte.

# Halo

My hair would make a pretty blaze,
a signal flare atop Mount Zion
burning for a thousand days,
outdazzling Venus and Orion.

A signal flare atop Mount Zion,
avatar of light-pollution
outdazzling Venus and Orion,
the full moon's sudden diminution.

Avatar of light-pollution
blotting out the Zodiac,
the full moon's sudden diminution
sending shivers down my back.

Blotting out the Zodiac,
Virgo, Libra, Capricorn,
sending shivers down my back:
Suppose I never had been born

because the sign of Capricorn
was darkened for a thousand days?
And if I never had been born
I couldn't set my hair ablaze.

# Indoor sports

I don't know why the dishwasher
doesn't want to play charades.
It grumbles at my attempts
to pose as a corkscrew. When I
scratch my ear with my foot
it immerses *The Last
Chronicle of Barset* in itself.

Last week I tried to teach it chess
and the silly thing danced
the Queen's Gambit around the block
leaving a rainbow trail of suds
and I had to call the SPCA
to come and take it to the zoo.

After it showed the wallaby
how to cheat at bezique, the alligator
filed for divorce and the otter
started plotting with the skink
to overthrow the government
and the zoocatcher called me and said
it wasn't working out.

So now we're back in the kitchen
playing Monopoly, and the dishwasher
has eaten all the grapefruit spoons,
and I'm struggling to collect $200
as I juggle a gross of greasy soup plates,
and the dishwasher is bored
and has gone back to absorbing
*Last Exit to Brooklyn.*

# Jamboree

O celebrate with kettledrums and curds
the seething Saturnalia of the stars,
awhile the whey from countless camel herds
lixiviates in Byzantine bazaars.
O cerebrate with cults and Tweedledums
anent the moon's fenestral apogee,
while though the brain's lacunae throbs and thrums
the antic pixilating jamboree.

And now our frenzy fades, and we enfold
ourselves in dying firelight, as we hear
the wrinkled bards and crones of yesteryear
reiterate the oddities of old,
until the dirge of tales told twice and thrice
consolidates our laughter into ice.

# Jeremiad

woe undo them
    that haven't the sundriest notion

woe undo berserkers
    cycling down the drainpipe of slough

woe undo them
    that don't know the next time round is acomin
    sooner than lickety splat on the prickly pavement

woe undo them
    that oughta know buns from gutter

woe undo them
    that run with the ginnels and snickets of fame
    and are wise in their own hindsight

woe undo the humorous
    sanguinary callers huddled under a bridge of phlegm

woe woe woe especially undo
    the comment-dire jesuses who nod knowingly
    and pour their spirits from the heights of fashion

woe now and woe then and
    play it again all those wowserish woes

# Legacy

A neverending shrug of obsolescence
pricks across the quondam-fruited plain.
Mute microorganisms toil amain
to deconstruct the litter of tumescence,
to bring again to its primordial essence
the wreckage of our reckless lust for gain.
A neverending shrug of obsolescence
pricks across the quondam-fruited plain.

Brassieres with built-in bioluminescence,
fluoridated hubcaps, all-terrain
refrigerators gessoed with cocaine—
To after-ages this was our quintessence:
a dead cacaphony of obsolescence
pricked and pricking, fruitless, on the plain.

# Little Plastic Hangers from New Pairs of Socks

I

little plastic hangers from new pairs of socks
decompressing behind closed doors
foster a fatal vanity

a hydraulic napkin dispenser
stable as a kettledrum
tries all men's patience and sobriety

the staleness of last year's cigar butt
looms thicker and whiter
than glib promises of progress

the gap-toothed grin of factories
morbid, self-indulgent, and misleading
evaporates like a bitter divorce

crumbling, leering gargoyles
arrive like a ballet at midnight
rife with aspic molds and giant stirring spoons

my wisest friend on the planet
sits in hollow trees and lonesome places
beset by intuitions of calamity

the id-monsters that rage through society
equipped for most eventualities including death and dentistry
stew, fry, boil, and bake

we live in a sea of carcinogens
we've frozen flexibility with profusion
like tangled wads of leftover yarn

shut up in unbelief
as unhappy as we are hopeless
our thumbs put out the sun

[*collage*: *Don Aslett, Adelle Davis, George Fox, Douglas Gwyn, Pauline Kael, Thomas Merton,* Philadelphia Inquirer *sports section, Ned Rorem, William Stringfellow*]

I I

This day is folded among the past,
the idea of time seems to curl up and fall asleep.
In the forbidden bliss of a sunlit laundry
these synthetic children of our restless hours—
a discordant hybrid of plant and of ghost—
lie so queer, at home in this jagged universe,
stone-silent in their innocent dark mindlessness
like bones sticking up out of the sand.
The essence of their style is languor,
a stern joy in astringency and desolation.

Through the stopped hole of an unwatched possibility
the skeleton blocking the path ahead,
uplifted and washed in the sun's crimson fidelity,
involuntarily rearranges itself
into an extension of petals in space.
An angel—a vortex of legs and arms—
mimics a tumbling pigeon.

Obstacles arc then like tissue-paper hoops.
A dread fanfare of music in the void
takes on a bright and caroling quality.
A policeman passes by leading the night on a leash;
against the shimmering backcloth of our dream
his shadow drops a curtsey.
Creators, harvesters and rejoicers tall with ecstasy
float and soar and sing
through the bright-hued windows of our sleep.

Bless the cup that wants to overflow.

[*collage: William James, Pauline Kael, Marion Milner, Vladimir Nabokov, Friedrich Nietzsche, Winifred Rawlins, J.R.R. Tolkien*]

III

Glory be to God for petty plastic
hawk-hooked holders of stretch socks—
handheld hairpin turns, Cinderella curlicues
sturdier than styrofoam, more solid than
shrinkwrap. I laud these lonely leftovers,
signs that no malign marketeers
have yet managed to make socks
seniorproof. Nor glitz nor glamor
disturbs their undergirding of the gold-toed
gloom which will launder into
an infinity of swart shades, each unique,
requisitions for a regiment of one
-legged legionnaires. The plastic bones
alone remain unlaved, their color constant:
ice skates for an outsized centipede.

# Longfellow Tells a Fib

And
now
here is
the poem
Fibonacci, the
syllables mounting and mounting,
making a pyramid, the difference in line lengths
wider and widening, until the structure becomes so unwieldy that it
      runs off the
page, and poor old Fibonacci must perforce collect his tables,
      Fibonacci number tables, and go home to Fibonicci-Gumi.

# Mammon his fourth commandment

remember the sabbath day and keep it wholly
commercial just like every other day
for if in the name of recalcitration
we aim to remake heaven and earth and sea and all that
into our own supersplendiferously virtual image
six out of seven are not enough

there is a monstrous spirit
which sniggers at evil left undone
there is a snide saccharine principle
which will commandeer any chink or cranny
that greed and selfishness forget to plug

rest for a single day
and up from under bushels and hogsheads
pops an eldritch crew of luminaries
withering the forest antennal with its glare

rest for a single hour and presto
uncreated is the blather
uncreated are the guns
uncreated is the whole polyestrial discotopia

heres what we gotta do
outrazzledazzle them glare them down
from every bathetic trident
let there be pyrotechnics
from each flat profitable bed perambulating the trackful wastes of
    old gloryland
unbutton the swell foop of a thousand thousand suns

dismember the sabbath day and keep it buried
we cant rest for a minute
with easter lacing the jelly beans
and banks of sperm dreaming of in vitro christmas

we havent a second to lose
59 out of 60 arent enough
364 out of 365 are not enough

# My Dream Conference

First, the accommodations:
The socially conscious wealthy
sleep in a boxcar with no mattresses
and draw their own water from a well.
I find a place in a dorm
for Bach lovers.

I've forgotten to bring my meds.
Someone is going to town.
I try to make a list,
but it seems that these days
all college-ruled paper comes
with automatic overwrite.

They're circulating a petition
printed on music paper;
but by the time I finish
composing my signature,
the petition has already
been delivered.

I check out the art exhibit.
All works containing a 4, 8, or 9
have been confiscated
under the Patriot Act.
The only thing on display
is a ratty old beach towel.

The day's activities conclude
with a guided meditation.
Given what I've seen so far
it comes as no surprise
that we are directed to use the mantra:
"Odd ... odd ... odd ...."

# My Last Duke

That's my last duke there hanging on the wall,
beside my diploma, under the neon sign.
Of course you see him pose with gun in hand,
shillelagh hanging fiercely from his belt,
fisherman's net slung over his right shoulder,
rope coiled nonchalantly around the left.
In his breast pocket (which doubles as an ashtray)
a swizzle stick. In short, the very picture
of *machismo*. Here's the sort of man, you'll say,
who braves the storm disdaining an umbrella,
who chomps on lemons, thinks a Rubik's cube
is something to chill a drink with, swings a scorpion
by the tail, deals bruises right and left,
and when he gets a windfall, treats the town
to pots of ale all round. Could you have seen him
in the privacy of his ducal chamber
shod in ballet shoes, toenails neatly clipped,
posed before the parabolic mirror
wearing a seashell necklace, all aslather
with perfume from an alabaster bottle,
dancing pagoda-hatted—then perhaps
you'd understand why MENE MENE TEKEL
UPHARSIN showed up, penciled on the wall
by an unseen hand, and why the sifters came
and winnowed him like chaff before the wind.

*(Challenge: list of 25 objects to be included)*

# Ode to a Creature seemingly incapable of Good

The Guinea-pig, or Restless Cavy. ....*They pass their whole Lives in sleeping, eating, and in the Propagation of their Species. They are by Nature gentle and tame; they do no Mischief, but seem to be equally incapable of Good.*
        —*William Bewick,* A General History of Quadrupeds, 1790

O restless Cavy! How canst thou be thinking
To cultivate Nobility of Mind,
Yet spend thy Days in eating, sleeping, drinking
And bootless Propagation of thy Kind?

"First do no Harm," commands the ancient Oath,
And while thou dost no Mischief, to be sure,
What Good can come of wallowing in Sloth,
Drowsing on Pine-chips mingled with Ordure?

Lo! beckons Pharmacology's Frontier!
Come, thou shalt brave unheard-of Tribulations!
Thine Exploits shall live on, O Pioneer,
Cited in scientific Publications.

O Pig, thou Inspiration for the Ages!
Whoso the Bounds of Probity o'erleap,
And Imbeciles, and Lunaticks in Cages,
From thee shall learn a Way to earn their Keep.

What though the Corporations get the Fame,
And Profits reap from Shore to distant Shore?
What though forgotten be thy private Name?
Thy Species shall become a Metaphor!

# Once the Spelljack

Once the spelljack has finished dangling
from the stone bridge over the gulch
and the melons have gone to their rest
under the eaves of silence,
then by a chainlinked happenstance
mercy's piebald horse will come at last
to roost in the hammock which Great-aunt May,
unbeholden to fashion's trammels, wove
from burgeons of milkweed and sedge.

Then will the melons awaken
plump with succulent psalms to spirits
nearer by far than any zeitgeist's
gaudy insinuations of urgency.
And mercy's piebald horse will neither
nicker nor neigh but will toss its quilted
mane in yeses of velvet.

# Orientation Speech

A compass
is an object about which it is not worth making a rumpus.
This wretched hunk of magnetite
can't even tell me which is my left hand and which is my right.
The location of north and south is a mystery which I have not the
    least interest in plumbing;
what I want to know is whether I'm going or coming.
Be so kind as to spare us
your lecture on the virtues of knowing the whereabouts of Polaris.
The wind bloweth where it listeth,
or so the Bible insisteth;
and what direction it bloweth from engageth me as little as how to
    tell splakes from wrasses.
Just give me a gadget that will point to where I put my glasses.

# Ostinato

*(Byr a thoddaid)*

Where is the air of yesteryear?
Where are the fields, fallow as deer?
They're gone, gone in a whorl of brine, to burn
until the rain turns alkaline.

Where are the snows of morrowmorn?
There high up on the Matterhorn
they dance, undecided which way to fall,
point and pirouette all the day.

Where are the stars of nevernight?
You cannot know, poor anchorite
who spurn the milk of skybridges unseen
for the glare of your mean fancies.

Hope remains, like a wire-wrapped string
that sends its ground bass pulsating
under the ever-shifting harmonies
drifting on the breeze from afar.

# Palynology

[*The study of "small, scattered things," i.e. fossil pollen, important to paleoclimatology.*]

Taoists
    are not to point at rainbows
    or spit at shooting stars.
This I heard in Sunday school when I was twelve.
Later I read the Psalms:
    "And may they be appalled by reason of their shame
    who say unto me, 'Aha! Aha!'"
Washington Irving's *Life of Mahomet*
yielded the danglingest participle of them all:
    "Having fallen into idolatry,
    God sent a prophet
    to restore them to the right way."

Flowers fade, the grasses wither.
The earthworm does its silent work
of making them one again
with the soil from which they came.
Only the grains of pollen abide,
indestructably buried
under the mulch of ages.
Who would sample a core,
who would go to such trouble
to watch them strut their hour upon the universal stage
talking about my adolescent weather?

The climate is different now.
Now I read (do I not?) with understanding.
Sirach was no Taoist:
    "Look at the rainbow,
    and praise him who made it."
Nor was Isaiah:

"How you are fallen from heaven,
    O Day Star, son of Dawn!
You are cast out like loathsome carrion,
    like a corpse trampled underfoot."

Yes, I read with maturer eyes.
I bring to the text
flashers. Floaters.
Zigzags glow around the edge.
Surely this is Truth.
But from deep within the core
reverberates the unheard overtone,
the Miocene echo:
    "You've fallen into idolatry, God!
    Ptui! Aha! Aha!"

# Panto

When I consider how my pants are rent—
bare ruined pants where late the sweet birds sang
(the silver swan, who living had no pants)—
pants fall apart; the center cannot hold.

Getting and spending, we lay waste our pants.
Pants, idle pants, I know not what they mean.
Thou still unravish'd pants of quietness
he fathers-forth whose trousers are past change.

# Paradelle: U.S. Congress and Copenhagen

There's no such thing as global warming.
There's no such thing as global warming.
Carbon dioxide is good for you.
Carbon dioxide is good for you.
Warming as carbon's nothing there
for you; such good is global dioxide.

Glaciers and ice are too much with us.
Glaciers and ice are too much with us.
The Eastern seaboard deserves to drown.
The Eastern seaboard deserves to drown.
Ice deserves the seaboard too much
and Eastern glaciers are to drown us with.

We can get natural gas out of rock.
We can get natural gas out of rock.
No one needs water; let them drink Coke.
No one needs water; let them drink Coke.
Let no one drink gas; Coke needs rock.
We can get them out of natural water.

There's ice deserves gas to let
the Eastern carbon rock for you.
Natural dioxide no can get with us
out of warming drowndrink no one needs.
We glaciers are such as waterboard them;
much sea is global Coke and good thing too.

# Plot with Epilog

Pale Polly and her pal Paul,
having splurged on pullets and pilchards,
pile onto a pillion, peel off
and splash through a pool of spilt pilsner.

Pyle the publicist
parlays this paltry exploit
into an explosion implicating
a pilaster, a pillarbox and a lightpole,
and unspools an implausible spiel
about pills, pallor, splinters and splints,
polyps, splayed spleens, epilepsy,
implants, transplants—
replete with public appeals
explicating the appalling plight
of these pulped pillars
of our plumeless bipedal populace.

Meanwhile Paul and Polly,
oblivious of their place in the plot,
pool their pelf
and get spliced in simple splendor.

# A Poem, Anyhow

Balderdash, he cried, shedding his toupee as he ran.
Furthermore, he panted, and jogged another mile.
Nevertheless, he sighed as he stepped off the scale.

He fell onto the sofa, martinis notwithstanding.
At any rate, he loathed the thought of paying taxes.
Moreover, he felt like the low man on the totem pole.

In the meantime, his children hid in the closet.

# The Powers Speak:

remember pearl harbor for now is the time for americans
to stand up and be counted we shall not be intimidated
fellow americans let us begin this historic and long
overdue crusade resolving to eradicate dissent from the
earth make the world understand that our government will
not be toyed with that what has happened is not to
be tolerated the american people must rise up as one we
must speak as one united voice in no uncertain terms we say
remember the alamo let other nations dread our might
for we are first among the countries of the world and we
intend to stay that way we have to defend our privilege
and the outrage americans suffered last tuesday will be
repaid a hundred times over at once with all the smartest
latest deadliest weapons in our arsenal for our innocent
blood is on someone else's hands no matter whose whoever
does not support total war may be assumed guilty and will
be made to pay we know god is on our side it is time to
fight terror with terror and remove the traitorous peaceniks
who threaten our freedoms our all-consuming American way
of life all true patriots are blind to what isnt on tv theres no
room here for lily-livered arrogance remember the maine

(November 2001)

# Progress

*(Homage to e e cummings)*

Pity this busy monster, manunkind, not progress;
or else misanthropy is what you'll find, not progress.

All hail the approaching bankruptcy of stars and stones!
Soon every square yard of land will be mined; what progress!

Translating littleness into ultraomnipotence,
"Perfection is what we're aiming for," they chime, "not progress."

Paperwork metastasizes, tears the flesh of time,
returns on its unself—a double bind, not progress.

Swaddled in cyberspace, death and life safely beyond,
icons of virtual violence are enshrined as progress.

Medicaments ensure a comfortable disease
and that no child shall be left behind in its progress.

Meanwhile and light years ago, the universe next door
pursues its far and wee ballooning, blind to progress.

All our comings and goings through curving wherewhen
mirror Sisyphean unwish, misdefined as progress.

# The Prophet

One day soon the sun
will be blotted out by a flock
of chickens the like of which
hasn't been seen since the days
of the passenger pigeon. The people
will weep and wail and rend
their garments. He alone
will be calm: *It's the chickens
coming home to roost.* And then
they will alight, trillions of them,
cadawking and cadoodling from every tree,
bush, rooftop, windowsill and telephone
wire, befouling the land; the stench
and the din will be unbearable—
but not for him: he will be able
to say, *I told you so.*

And he'll strut around in his pride,
a cruel fire in his eyes, and meanwhile
the people will have left
off wailing and will be dancing
and singing, "Oh, we'll kill
the old red rooster when she comes...,"
and all over the land there will be
bonfires and merriment and the aroma
of roast chicken, and he alone
will be aloof, stalking through
the darkness with glittering
haunted eyes, muttering:
*I told you so, I told you so....*

# Psalm MCMLXXXIV

My God, your forthright glory is exceeding,
    your light will not be hid.
Never one to whimper forth a cosmos
    you rupture earth and sidewalk, amnion and eggshell
    with your relentless burgeoning.

You have heard it sung of old:
Manifold are your works, O God!
    The earth is full, full of your riches!
Can you not take a hint?
Spare me the riot of your importunate birthing
    for just a little while.
Show me a land where night unto night
    uttereth sweet nothings
    instead of unremitting whelps of joy.

Many a time have I cried aloud unto you, "Enough!
    Enough!"
    And for answer you delivered me.
Tell me, indomitable midwife,
    where by law or prophet is it written that we must be born again
    and again
    and yet and yet again?

# "Reification Won't Get You Out of the Parking Lot"

*(Descort on a line by Bob Perelman)*

Reification won't get you
out of the parking lot.
Don't expect on-the-spot
relief from woes that beset you.
Idolization won't net you
blessings from gods who are not.
Reification won't get you
out of the parking lot.

Amassing of things won't let you
be content with diddley-squat.
True peace of mind is what,
whether you're clingy or macho,
reification won't get you.

\*

Blackboard
        with serried fingernails,
Dark desert with rocks
        that move of themselves,
Bubbly tar pit adding its fetid breath
        to the summer swelter—
Our world.
        Our home.
                Our tomb.

\*

Ray's vacation
woe and kachoo
oh what a poor kinglet

\*

Higgledy piggledy
poor Bobby Perelman
stuck in a parking lot
day after day;
if he'd adopt an un-
reificational
view of the cosmos, he'd
be on his way.

\*

"Reification" is a word which you
won't find in poetry  The reader just wouldn't
get it. Why in the whole wet world would
you use it? You'd have to be
out of touch with the whole idea
of what poetry is *for*, what poetry *is*,
the quintessential thing-ness of the poetic project, to go
parking such a word in the midst of a
lot of real words that can get along perfectly well without it.

\*

Hear their mournful song!
O how they long
for sweet release
from earthly bonds.
Would we could
zap, dematerialize,
vaporize, uninvent
those hapless vehicles
stranded on the concrete,
send them off into
glad abstraction,
no longer doomed

to be mere pale copies
of the ideal automobile.
But since such blessed
liberation is not within
our power, alas! a lack
of parking is our lot.

\*

How proudly we dishonor the worth of new life,
try our utmost to create a dearth of new life.

For us to succeed in making ourselves extinct
might well be the best way to further new life.

We pour our toxins out into air, water, land
as if we thought nothing could be worse than new life.

God gave us dominion over the beasts and plants,
but he didn't mean that as a curse on new life.

Ever since the Mississippian period
cockroaches have been giving birth to new life.

Newborn rats rest side by side on my palm,
twin pink grubs of little-finger girth: new life.

From sulfurous vent in the deepest ocean trench
to puddle, arroyo, geyser, firth—new life.

Give over your mad accumulation of things
and open your soul to genuine mirth: new life.

The energizing spirit's medium of exchange
lies outside our frantic world of commerce: new life.

Hope, relentless, insinuates green leaves through
cracks in the parking lot: from the earth, new life.

# Rondel on Lines by James Tate

Knit the mosquitoes together
beneath your pajamas.
Leave all your mammas
gamboling in the heather;
enclose the words you blether
in inverted commas,
and knit the mosquitoes together
beneath your pyjamas.

What does it matter whether
you find three-L lllamas
in postmodern dramas?
Take a long thong of leather
and knit the mosquitoes together.

(*Refrain lines from James Tate, "Recipe for sleep"*)

# St. Swithin's Day 2003

No rain for St. Swithin today.
It's so hot the road is melting.
With a key borrowed from the warden
we let ourselves into the little church.
The earth was flat when it was built,
the sky a dome, sealing off heaven beyond.

The wall paintings of the Last Judgment,
somewhat the worse for centuries
of hiding under Puritan whitewash,
fail to dispel our sense of peace.
Nor do the faded ochres and reds
belie the welcome coolness of this place.

The church library—leather-bound,
massive, musty—is chained to the wall:
one New Testament paraphrase,
plus the tome of readymade sermons
imposed by fiat of Elizabeth I.
We won't be back with bolt cutters.

Out by the road, we find ourselves
become as little children;
bending down with one accord
(sixty years ago we would have
hunkered), we each punch
a bubble in the asphalt.

# Sanctuary

Look at it this way: If we could
consign the Bush League
to the depths of the ocean trenches,
there to spend eternity mired in
graywacke, under excruciating pressure
in water superheated from the mantle
to 700 degrees Fahrenheit,
breathing rotten-egg gas—then

they'd promptly set about destroying
the giant tube worms, giant clams,
spider crabs, and most especially those
creatures unlike anything we know—
denizens of an alternate biosphere
whose very being engenders
an eerie hope.

# Sea Pork

[*Colonial hemichordates, distant precursors of the vertebrates*]

You see our peaceful colony
as a pinky-yellow oblong on the rocks.
Thinking we are a bar of soap
you stoop to pick us up, and when your hand
meets not firm smoothness
but squishy flesh, you flinch.

And then you think: What novel
kind of lorelei is this that lures
the unsuspecting with a promise
of instant whiter-than-whiteness?

Soap by its very rhyme
engenders hope. Exiles
from the primordial oneness
yearn to be made clean
forever.

But we never promised you ablution.
We are merely waiting for the tide
to return us to our native element
before you figure out a way
to market us.

# Shine, Perishing Republic

Shine, perishing republic
like a rotten mackerel by moonlight.
Obese with empire, choking
on the reflux of greed, we flounder
in the muck of our own making.

An emergency protest
crams a vest-pocket park
named for a jailed state senator.
A bubble in the sludge
plops and fizzles.

# Sifter

Well, if you ever need a lift,
just grab your sifter and sift and sift.
Sift the sugar, sift the flour,
sift for a minute, sift for an hour,

sift until the sun has set,
jiggle the handle like a castanet.
Jiggle that handle loud and louder,
sift the salt and baking powder,

sift the cornmeal, sift the bran
sift as much as ever you can.
And as you sift, dance round and round,
making tracks all over the ground.

No more flour? Go to the store,
rip open their bags and sift some more.
Take your sifter wherever you go,
and your fame will grow and grow.

Sift for better, sift for worse,
winnow the whole wide universe
until in Heaven they'll entrust you
with the job of sifting the cosmic dust.

# So there, Robert Bly!

*Robinson Jeffers is a man with an extremely powerful mammal brain, in whom, nevertheless, the reptile brain had a slight edge. His magnificent poems are not warm toward human beings. On the contrary, he has a curious love for the claw and the most ancient sea rocks. – Robert Bly,* Leaping Poetry

My poetry is reptilian and less than reptilian,
full of geckoes, axolotls, rollerblading snakes,
skinks, splakes, slugs of land and sea,
sea pork imitating soap, trilobites imitating pecans,
merry calimari, concertina-playing clams,
bonellia husbands swapping yarns inside their wife,
centipedes doing tai chi, fireflies blinking red.

My poetry is mammalian, full of capybaras,
guinea pigs dauntful and heroic,
mountain sheep winding their horns,
luminous puppies, unemployed aardvarks,
horses roosting in hammocks, plummeting hyraxes,
weeping wombats, polecats searching for Wednesday,
paleohippus and Smilodon the smiling don.

My poetry is objective, full of amorous mailcarts,
card-playing dishwashers, breakdancing tables,
wailing sprockets, selfish pulleys, sinister awls,
U-bolts crocheting patriotic songs,
somnolent rubies, stalwart pajamas,
time-traveling oranges—
but now we're getting into botany.

Avast, ye neurotypicals!
I won't play your game of "heads and bodies."
I'm not about to trade this old encephalon
for a skull replete with warmest fuzzies
to suit your newbrained notions
of what a right and proper poem should be.

# Sylviade

Deep in the woods   where the deer dwell,
skunks scrunch   over last year's cones,
and foxes fleer   at ferns underfoot
where shrews unnoticed   scurry and scold.

When the wind rises   the white pines whistle
while grosbeaks gawk   at their resinous gunk.
Yews yearn   for yesterday's drizzle,
willows await   the williwaw.

At dawn the woods   awakes with wonder,
"Hallelujah,"   hymn the hornbeams.
Junipers join in:   "Jubilate."
The whole forest   lifts up its voice.

The trees trot out   their hidden talents:
Aspens compete   in a quaking contest,
larches collude   to produce lemons,
and on the horizon   hemlocks hover.

Deep in the woods   the dusk descends;
oaks coax   their acorns to sleep.

# Thanksgiving

My browser is taking a poll:
What are you most thankful for?

    a)    turkey

    b)    football

    c)    shopping

For the turkey
whose mana we ingest
so that we too
can be stuffed
to immobility
and impotence
let us be virtually thankful.

For images of stylized mayhem
with arbitrary rules
which we can safely
watch from our roost
pretending that
the outcome matters
let us be virtually thankful.

For the stream of clutter
which gives our lives
meaning and helps us
outgrow our coops
let us be virtually thankful.

For protection from a world
with real anguish
and real mourning
and maybe even repentance
not to mention
blessings worth counting
let us be virtually thankful.

# To a Table

*"Mensa, O table, is vocative case," he replied. "You would use it in speaking to a table."*
*"But I never do," I blurted out in honest amazement.*
*—Winston Churchill's memoirs*

Now listen, table. We're having company
for dinner. You'll have an extra leaf,
so tighten your stomach muscles;
no sagging. And don't complain. Forget
that folderol about a groaning board.

Instead of your usual junk-shop chic
you'll wear a *birqa*. None of your
Marie Antoinette headdresses
flaunting piles of paper in artful dishabille.
And no *tabula rasa* act either.

Another thing: Stand still.
No can-can, Charleston, Irish jig,
break-dancing. No pretending to be
an octopus, spooking the guests
by coiling around their legs.

It's time you learned to be
a disinclined plane without
playing the martyr. Just try
to be civilized for once, and set
a good example for the chairs.

# 21$^{st}$-Century American Cutup

This is the hour of the great contempt.
Seven-headed business
gropes groundwards with grisly arms
and flame-coloured teeth,
wanting to eat a landscape.

A government unworthy of credence or trust
dribbles and dawdles on the perimeter,
asking no ultimate questions.
Cravens at council crow proudly with the hearts of hens,
making solemn leagues and countenances.

Dislocation is eroticized;
superabundant stars
stir souls with false prophecies,
sunny rot and corruption,
a storm of drunken joy.

There is ice in their laughter,
the unnerving cold ominousness
of dead things shamming life
in an animated cartoon by Hieronymus Bosch.
The world withers and the wind rises.

[*Collage: Douglas Gwyn, Pauline Kael, Thomas Merton, Marion Millner, Vladimir Nabokov, Friedrich Nietzsche,* Philadelphia Inquirer *sports section, Winifred Rawlins, W.C. Sellar and R.J. Yeatman, William Stringfellow, J.R.R. Tolkien, John Greenleaf Whittier, Tennessee Williams*]

# The Two Prophets

*(Jeremiah 28:1-17)*

Jeremiah wore a wooden yoke
around his neck, made of the stoutest oak.
"Babylon will hold in thrall our folk
     for years to come."

Hananiah said to him, "Our men
will be in Babylon and out again,
victorious, before you count to ten.
     It'll be a romp."

Said Jeremiah, "When we no longer pour
men and money into this foreign war,
when we depend on our own might no more,
     I'll know you're right."

Then stepped Hananiah up and broke
from Jeremiah's neck the wooden yoke,
and cock-a-hoop these gloating words he spoke:
     "Mission accomplished!"

Jeremiah held himself in check
and went away awhile. When he came back
he had an iron yoke around his neck.
     Told Hananiah:

"You have broken off the yoke of wood,
but now we'll wear a yoke of iron for good,
sending our riches and our livelihood
     to Babylon.

"You have condemned this nation by your lie
to endless servitude. I prophesy

that before the year is out you'll die,
    your name accursed."

And sure enough, as Jeremiah swore,
Hananiah died and was no more,
He left behind a greedy, pointless war—
    his country ruined.

And did the people mend their wanton ways
and listen to Jeremiah all their days?
What happened next? Well, that's another phase,
    another story.

# Unjubilee

*(Leviticus 25)*

this is the year   of the unjubilee
bandersnatch rampant   on a sinister bent
grimereapers spew   the noisome spoil
    of the unjubilee

landlubbers flee   the clutchhold's snarl
parchmen conspire   to corner the rain
airmongers suit   the world to the deeds
    of the unjubilee

doomyeast leavens   the badyear blimp
a flaming oil rig   scolds the sky
the moon limps off   to the lazaret
    of the unjubilee

# Unglobed Fruit

Two oranges
times two oranges
make four square oranges.
These, neither palpable
nor mute, gibber at gawkers
from their prison under glass,
then slip behind the frame
to multiply in private.

Sixteen time-traveling oranges,
cube edges blurred, hop
from recollection to foreboding,
sample mud and medallions
in a jagged tour
of fossil tracks and unbuilt skyroads
zagging from whimper
to bang.

Their two hundred fifty-six offspring
hurtle outward past the climbing
of the moon, speed on the solar wind,
warp beyond spacetime
to that nowhen where a throbbing
googolplex of rhymed oranges
implode into a syzygy
of poem : mean : be.